Sioux City Memories

The Early Years • A Pictorial History

presented by

ACKNOWLEDGMENTS

The Sioux City Journal is pleased to present "Sioux City Memories: The Early Years." It must be noted, however, that this unique pictorial history book would not have been possible without the generous contributions made by many people from virtually every corner of our community.
We are indebted, first of all, to those early area residents who captured their time — our history — in photographs, and provided a glimpse into their lives.
Secondly, all area residents are indebted to the many individuals who are committed to preserving our history in various libraries, historical societies, archives and personal collections throughout our community.

The following organization has contributed greatly to this project:
Sioux City Museum & Historical Association

BEGINNING THE STORY

When The Sioux City Journal printed its first paper – Aug. 20, 1864 – readers were given an update on the Civil War.

"War matters are about at a standstill," the newspaper reported. "Nothing is being done by either army."

The Journal, however, proudly declared itself a "Union" newspaper and aligned with President Abraham Lincoln who, it said, was having problems with Democrats in the North and rebels in the South. To prove as much, the second edition listed members of the country's executive branch and insisted it was not intended to be a "Republican or an Abolition or a Copperhead organ."

Advertisers also got on the bandwagon: "Down with the Rebs and with high prices," the Cheap, Cash Store insisted.

Poetry, jokes and stories from other newspapers filled the rest of the four pages. Attorneys, physicians and tailors advertised. The United States Mail Line promised it could get mail in two days from Sioux City to Fort Dodge.

Life sprang from the black-and-white type. Incorporated in 1857, Sioux City was in its infancy, but filled with promise.

The city's name, of course, came from the Sioux tribe and the Big Sioux River. It had been a stopping point for the Lewis and Clark Expedition. Coincidentally, the visit came 60 years to the day before The Journal started printing. Charles Floyd, a sergeant in the U.S. Army, died Aug. 20, 1804, and was buried atop a bluff near Sioux City that later bore his name.

The "restless and turbid waters of the Missouri," according to one report, cut away the bluff taking parts of the grave with it. A committee worked to repair it, return the contents and create a monument in Floyd's honor. In May 1901, the Floyd Monument was dedicated.

Those intervening years, however, proved crucial to the area. It was a time of settling in, planting roots and creating homes.

In 1865, Sioux City received $20,000 to build a wagon bridge across the Big Sioux River. Two thousand dollars was spent to survey the area and determine what materials were needed. The rest of the money disappeared. The bridge wasn't built. A time of innocence had ended.

The newspaper, meanwhile, continued to do as it set out – to chronicle the times, write an active history and let others know what mattered.

"We come among you, as any business, to pursue our calling and to make a living," the editor wrote on that first day.

For him – and us – the story was about to unfold.

TABLE OF CONTENTS

CHAPTER ONE

VIEWS AND STREET SCENES

While Native Americans called the area home for thousands of years, Sioux City was a magnet for East Coast residents looking for a new way of life in the 1800s.

French fur trader Theophile Bruguier, dubbed the "first white settler in Sioux City," built a cabin in 1849 that indicated outsiders were ready to stay. Other businesses and homes arrived, attracted to the transportation opportunities afforded by the Missouri River. By 1866, Pearl Street boasted several businesses. A "downtown" area had begun.

Steamboats made regular stops in the late 1800s; visitors put Sioux City on their itinerary.

A huge draw in those early days: The Sioux City Corn Palace. Thankful for an abundance harvest (and an end to drought and grasshopper invasions), residents decided to hold a festival and corn jubilee. That prompted talk of building a corn palace, not unlike the ice palace constructed in St. Paul. Residents rallied and the first was ready in 1887. It attracted President Grover Cleveland and railroad officials who indicated that "Sioux City has everything in which railroads are interested." Four more corn palaces rose between 1888 and 1891. Another was planned but financial woes forced the city to scrap construction and Mitchell, South Dakota, picked up the idea in 1892 and has held a festival ever since. Sioux City, though, was considered the innovator – a designation that helped foster a vibrant downtown throughout the early part of the 20th century.

Fires and floods may have threatened portions of the city's existence, but citizens' determination insisted it was worth rebuilding.

OPPOSITE: A view of Fourth Street looking east from Pierce Street, circa 1925. COURTESY SIOUX CITY MUSEUM

RIGHT: Pearl Street looking north from the corner of Second Street, Sioux City, 1866. This was Sioux City's original downtown. COURTESY SIOUX CITY MUSEUM

BELOW RIGHT: Entrance to the 1888 Corn Palace, northeast corner of Sixth and Pierce streets, Sioux City. COURTESY SIOUX CITY MUSEUM

BELOW: Steamboats on the Missouri River levy looking southeast from the Sawyers Block at Second and Pearl streets, Sioux City, 1869. COURTESY SIOUX CITY MUSEUM

ABOVE: The Corn Palace, northeast corner of Sixth and Pierce streets, Sioux City, 1889. The Woodbury County Courthouse is on the right. COURTESY SIOUX CITY MUSEUM

ABOVE LEFT: Bird's eye view of Pearl Street, Sioux City, 1868. COURTESY SIOUX CITY MUSEUM

LEFT: The 1891 Corn Palace, Sixth and Pierce streets, Sioux City. This was the last of Sioux City Corn Palaces. COURTESY SIOUX CITY MUSEUM

ABOVE: Sioux City Grocery, 200 Fourth St., Sioux City, about 1892. COURTESY SIOUX CITY MUSEUM

LEFT: City Scales on Water Street, Sioux City, about 1895. COURTESY SIOUX CITY MUSEUM

OPPOSITE TOP LEFT: Fourth Street view of Sergeants Bluff, 1909. COURTESY RAYMOND LEFEBVERE

OPPOSITE TOP RIGHT: Fourth Street looking east from Pierce Street (just prior to the arrival of the automobile), Sioux City, 1900. COURTESY SIOUX CITY MUSEUM

OPPOSITE BOTTOM LEFT: Fourth Street looking east from Douglas Street, Sioux City, 1908. Note the electric streetcar. The street was not dirt, but paved with cedar blocks. COURTESY SIOUX CITY MUSEUM

OPPOSITE BOTTOM RIGHT: Fourth Street looking east from Pierce Street, shortly after electrification of Sioux City's streetcar system, 1891. COURTESY SIOUX CITY MUSEUM

LEFT: Pelletier fire scene, looking east on Fourth Street from Pierce Street, Sioux City, 1904. The fire destroyed about two-and-a-half blocks of downtown, causing $2 million in damage. COURTESY SIOUX CITY MUSEUM

FAR LEFT: Third and Douglas streets looking east, Sioux City, about 1910. COURTESY JOE STABILE

OPPOSITE: Fourth Street view, Sioux City, about 1908. COURTESY SIOUX CITY MUSEUM

BELOW LEFT: Pelletier fire scene, looking northeast from Third and Nebraska Streets, Sioux City, 1904. COURTESY SIOUX CITY MUSEUM

BELOW: Firemen work to put out the Brown Block Fire, Sioux City business district, 1914. COURTESY BERNIE ATTEMA

RIGHT AND BELOW: Brown Block fire, Sioux City, March 1914. Firefighters Frank Fulton and Seeley Layton perished in the fire. COURTESY SIOUX CITY MUSEUM

OPPOSITE TOP LEFT: A busy day at the West Hotel, Third and Nebraska streets, Sioux City, 1912. COURTESY BERNIE ATTEMA

OPPOSITE TOP RIGHT: Robert J. McIntyre in his family's front yard at 3110 Jones St., Sioux City, about 1916. The tree pictured here still stands. COURTESY MARILYN MCINTYRE CHADWICK

OPPOSITE BOTTOM LEFT: Street view looking west on Fourth Street from Pierce Street, Sioux City, circa 1915. Davidson Brothers Department Store is on the left. COURTESY SIOUX CITY MUSEUM

OPPOSITE BOTTOM RIGHT: Continental Bank in the Iowa Building at the southwest corner of Fifth and Pierce streets, Sioux City, about 1917. COURTESY SIOUX CITY MUSEUM

THIS PAGE AND OPPOSITE: The Ruff disaster, one of Sioux City's biggest disasters, north-east corner of Fourth and Douglas, June 29, 1918. The building was being remodeled but collapsed during the remodeling which then caused a fire. Thirty-seven people were killed. COURTESY SIOUX CITY MUSEUM

RIGHT: First National Bank at the northwest corner of Fifth and Pierce streets, Sioux City, about 1920. COURTESY SIOUX CITY MUSEUM

BELOW RIGHT: A delivery truck and driver sit in front of Headington and Hedenbergh Company, 200 Pearl Street, Sioux City, about 1920. The company was a wholesale fruit and vegetable company. The building was eventually torn down to make room for the Stoney Creek Inn. COURTESY SIOUX CITY MUSEUM

BELOW: Exterior of the Sioux City Journal, southwest corner of Fifth and Douglas streets, about 1916. COURTESY SIOUX CITY MUSEUM

ABOVE: W.W. Orcutt house, 1726 Grandview Blvd. (originally known as 1720 Pearl St.), Sioux City, about 1920. W.W. Orcutt owned the first hardware store in downtown Sioux City at 312-314 Nebraska St. COURTESY PEARL ORCUTT AUSTIN FAMILY

LEFT: Street view of the Orcutt Building, 314 Nebraska St., Sioux City, 1920s. COURTESY PEARL ORCUTT AUSTIN FAMILY

BELOW: Panoramic view of three houses on Morningside Avenue looking west from 4510 Morningside, Sioux City, 1922. COURTESY DEAN AND PATRICIA SHEEHAN

LEFT: Fourth Street looking west from Jones, Sioux City, circa 1915. COURTESY BERNIE ATTEMA

OPPOSITE: Looking east on Fourth Street from the Martin Hotel at Fourth and Pierce streets, Sioux City, 1920. COURTESY SIOUX CITY MUSEUM

BELOW LEFT: The Thorvald Andersen family visiting grave site of Sgt. Floyd, Floyd Monument, Sioux City, 1924. COURTESY ERIC GEORGESEN

BELOW RIGHT: The Orpheum Vaudeville Theater, downtown Sioux City at 414 Nebraska St., 1920s. The theater was originally built as the Capitol and was home of the Orpheum circuit. It opened in 1918 and closed in the 1960s. COURTESY SIOUX CITY MUSEUM

ABOVE: Sixth Street view, Sioux City, about 1935. COURTESY SIOUX CITY MUSEUM

RIGHT: This photo shows distraught depositors milling around the Sioux National Bank located at the corner of Fourth and Pierce Streets, Sioux City, 1930. The bank folded on Dec. 6, 1930. Eventually depositors received a portion of their investment back. The bank sat empty until all remaining assets were sold in a receiver's sale on Feb. 14, 1936. COURTESY SIOUX CITY MUSEUM

ABOVE: This 1936 photo shows the double log cabin that was built in 1849 by Theophile Bruguier. The cabin is a rectangular single story one-room house with a gable roof. The logs are hand-hewn and are kept together by chinking as a French-style log cabin. It was rediscovered in 1933 by the Rev. John Hantla and moved to Riverside Park the following year. The Sioux City Council set aside the cabin for use by The Girls of '68 Junior Pioneers in 1936. COURTESY GIRLS OF '68/DIANE GARDNER

LEFT: Street view of the 1934 flood, 2805 Rebecca St., Sioux City. This house was the only house on the street that did not flood. COURTESY PATRICIA LAMOUREUX

FAR LEFT: Holiday shoppers in front of Kresge Company 5 and 10 store, corner of Fourth and Pierce streets, Sioux City, mid-1930s. COURTESY JOE STABILE

CHAPTER TWO

TRANSPORTATION

Horses, trains, boats, cars and planes.

Lewis and Clark knew the Missouri River was crucial to accessing the Great Plains. But businessmen soon discovered it, too, and realized it was key to connecting one part of the area to another. Natural and man-made transportation routes are the most significant factors in the building and development of a city.

The first people came to Sioux City on horseback or by stagecoach, up the Missouri River Valley. Sioux City was also a popular stop for river traffic and the Sioux City Townsite Co. chartered the first steamboat delivery aboard the "Omaha" in 1856.

The iron rails of the Sioux City & Pacific Railroad were laid to the city in the late 1860s and the first train arrived on March 9, 1868. Because of Sioux City's geographically significant location on the Missouri River, the city became the Steamboat Capital of the Upper Missouri. Other railroad companies built to and from Sioux City, and by 1929 Sioux City was the 10th largest railroad center in the United States.

As far back as the 1860s, bridging the Missouri River was a business priority. Approval was granted by the U.S. Congress in 1872, but no bridge was completed until the opening of the Missouri River Railroad Bridge on Dec. 5, 1888. Other bridges followed, like the Combination Bridge, for both rail and pedestrian traffic which opened in 1896.

New technologies in the 20th century like the automobile and airplane also had a tremendous impact on Sioux City. Dozens of automobile dealerships opened. Sioux City businesses began manufacturing automobile parts, like trunks, tires and even whole trucks. The Kari-Keen Manufacturing Co. built airplanes and, by the 1930s, three airfields were operating in and around Sioux City.

OPPOSITE: Division Street Station of the Sioux City Rapid Transit Company's elevated railroad, circa 1892. COURTESY SIOUX CITY MUSEUM

ABOVE: Corn Palace promotional train headed for Washington, D.C., from Sioux City, 1889. The train was heading to Washington to promote visiting Sioux City's Corn Palace. COURTESY JOE STABILE

RIGHT: The Benton, Western, Nellie Peck and Far West steamboats lined up at the Sioux City levy, Missouri River, about 1870. COURTESY SIOUX CITY MUSEUM

ABOVE: Locomotive and cars of the surface line of the elevated railroad, Morningside, 1888. COURTESY SIOUX CITY MUSEUM

LEFT: Horse-drawn buggy on the ungraded hills of the north side, Sioux City, about 1890. COURTESY SIOUX CITY MUSEUM

ABOVE AND RIGHT: The Jones Street Station of the elevated railroad, 1891. The company operating the line was the Sioux City Rapid Transit Company. COURTESY SIOUX CITY MUSEUM

ABOVE: The steam stern-wheeler snag boat James B. McPherson pulling snags in the vicinity of the Sioux City Boat Club, Sioux City, late 1890s. COURTESY SIOUX CITY MUSEUM

ABOVE LEFT: The Power House of the Sioux City Cable Railway Company, Sioux City, 1890. The company operated the Sioux City Cable Car line from 1888 to 1893. COURTESY SIOUX CITY MUSEUM

LEFT: Horse-drawn bus of the Sioux City Bus Line in front of the Garretson Hotel at Fifth and Pierce streets, Sioux city, circa 1890. COURTESY SIOUX CITY MUSEUM

ABOVE: The Montgomery Ward Company electric horseless carriage, passing through Sioux City, about 1901. COURTESY SIOUX CITY MUSEUM

ABOVE LEFT: Electric streetcars lined up on Fourth Street, at the intersection on Pearl Street, 1896. COURTESY SIOUX CITY MUSEUM

LEFT: Horse-drawn buckboard at the H. Fachman barn, Sioux City, circa 1900. COURTESY SIOUX CITY MUSEUM

OPPOSITE: Crewmembers of the Sioux City and Leeds Electric Railway pose in the car barn located in Leeds, 1908. Identified: Ray Rubel is fourth from left. COURTESY SIOUX CITY MUSEUM

ABOVE: Charles Coacher was an engineer for Milwaukee Railroad out of Sioux City, 1910s. COURTESY KAY AND BOB COACHER

ABOVE RIGHT: Chicago Northwestern passenger depot, at Second and Nebraska streets, Sioux City, 1920s. COURTESY SIOUX CITY MUSEUM

RIGHT: A customer picking up an order at the Palmer Fruit Company, Sioux City, circa 1915. Palmer Fruit at 210 Pearl St. was in business from 1878 to 1969. This building was built in 1914 (later torn down to make room for the hotel) and had special banana curing rooms, produce coolers, and humidity-controlled storage areas. COURTESY PALMER CANDY COMPANY

ABOVE: C.S. Hollman Livery and Boarding Stable, 607 Douglas St., Sioux City, about 1907. Note the Sturges Brothers saddle blanket on the horse. Charles L. and Ernest F. Sturges were harness makers and dealers in Sioux City from 1888 to 1941. This photo was taken at the current location of the police station. COURTESY SIOUX CITY MUSEUM

ABOVE LEFT: This car is parked on the stairs of Sioux City High School, 1908. Photo was used as an ad for Carter Cars. Mr. Edmonds, driving; E.L. Adams, center; and Tracy G. Hall. COURTESY SIOUX CITY MUSEUM

MIDDLE LEFT: The first delivery van for Palmer Candy, Sioux City, about 1920. This shiny new REO Truck is shown parked in front of the REO dealership. Of special interest is the driver's name, Earl Bower, which is proudly listed on the door in the style of the fighter planes from that same era. COURTESY PALMER CANDY COMPANY

LEFT: E & W Clothing delivery truck, Fourth Street, Sioux City, 1918. The driver and passenger are unidentified. COURTESY ST. PAUL'S LUTHERAN CHURCH/BERNIE ATTEMA

RIGHT: Hawkeye truck loaded with beer, Sixth and Nebraska streets, Sioux City, circa 1914. Prohibition in Iowa started in 1916.
COURTESY BERNIE ATTEMA

FAR RIGHT: Scene of a car crash at a railroad crossing, Sioux City, 1925.
COURTESY GRACE CALHOUN KAVANAUGH

BELOW RIGHT: A four-passenger airplane at Leeds Airport, 1927. Front row, from left: unidentified, T. Toval and Al Anderson. Back row, from left: Ralph Tappan, Warren Anderson, Harold Tennant, Shorty Leckscheid, Ray Fuller and Mr. & Mrs. Joe Russel. The airport was short-lived and was gone by the early 1930s. COURTESY SIOUX CITY MUSEUM

ABOVE: A fleet of delivery trucks and drivers for the Galinsky Brothers Company, Sioux City, 1935. The company was a fruit wholesaler. COURTESY SIOUX CITY MUSEUM

LEFT: John Cheever standing next to his delivery truck, Sioux City, 1930s. John worked and delivered magazines and newspapers for the Olson News Company.
COURTESY CAROLYN J. COUGHLIN

FAR LEFT: Syl Cusack's new delivery trucks for The Capitol Laundry parked in front of the Harold Hathaway Company, on Fifth Street, between Jennings and Virginia streets, Sioux City, early 1930s.
COURTESY KAY AND BOB COACHER

CHAPTER THREE

COMMERCE

Wherever people gather, businesses are sure to follow.
That was true in the 1800s. It's true today.

After the Sioux City Townsite Company was formed in 1854, the sale of lots began. Streets were staked later that year and over the next two years, a bank, hotels, a post office and a government land office opened. Homes sprouted along the river.

The Pacific Railroad arrived in 1868 and transformed the town.

Thanks to access by boat, Sioux City, one historian said, became the "steamboat capital of the West," usurping St. Louis.

By 1870, more than 4,000 people called the place home. Four grain elevators sprang up, a lumberyard appeared and five farm implement dealers were in business. James E. Booge, a wholesale grocer and government pork contractor, constructed the city's first substantial hog slaughtering and processing plant and the city's identity began to take shape. Workers flocked to the city in record numbers. The future looked bright and, then, a nationwide financial panic hit in 1893 and Sioux City began to suffer.

Because many businesses were in their infancy, they couldn't survive and, as a result, they and their employees left. More than 20,000 people exited between 1893 and 1895. The key to turning things around, leaders said, was completion of the Combination Bridge. The Credits Commutation Company led the charge, organized the Sioux City Stock Yards Company, created the Live Stock National Bank and attracted Armour and Company to purchase the former Silberhorn/Anglo-American/International packing plant. The cloud had been lifted, thanks to the tenacity of business leaders.

In the next decade, Sioux City would regain in standing as the second largest city in Iowa. Stores flourished and the stage was set for even more growth.

OPPOSITE: Customers and staff of Bartels Cafe located at 426 Sixth St., Sioux City, late 1930s. Charles Bartels was the proprietor. COURTESY SIOUX CITY MUSEUM

ABOVE: Owner James Finnegan and patrons of the Northern Exchange Saloon, 211 Douglas St., Sioux City, 1891. COURTESY SIOUX CITY MUSEUM

RIGHT: The Fair Drygoods Company, 320 Fourth St., Sioux City, 1889. Eugene H. Gilmore proprietor.
COURTESY SIOUX CITY MUSEUM

OPPOSITE: The Washington House Hotel, 510 Pearl St., Sioux City, circa 1905. George Schlupp is on the far right. The Federal Building is currently located on this site.
COURTESY CAROL BIRMINGHAM STRAIT

ABOVE: John Roschitsch Saloon, Sioux City, about 1910. Roschitsch is standing behind the counter on the left side, Joseph Peschel is behind the bar on the right side. COURTESY SIOUX CITY MUSEUM

ABOVE RIGHT: Guenther Wholesale Toys and Notions, 315 Fourth St., Sioux City, circa 1895. Anton Guenther proprietor. COURTESY SIOUX CITY MUSEUM

RIGHT: Chesterman and Lane Bottlers delivery wagon, Sioux City, about 1895. The company was located at 15th and Omaha streets.
COURTESY SIOUX CITY MUSEUM

ABOVE: Weare and Allison Bank, 405 Pearl St., Sioux City, 1895. This was Sioux City's first bank, established in the 1850s. The building pictured here was built in 1878. COURTESY SIOUX CITY MUSEUM

ABOVE LEFT: Guenther Wholesale Toys and Notions, 315 Fourth St., Sioux City, circa 1895. Anton Guenther proprietor. COURTESY SIOUX CITY MUSEUM

LEFT: Schwinn Grocer delivery wagon, Sioux City, about 1895. The wagon is a Dineen Wagon, built in Sioux City. COURTESY SIOUX CITY MUSEUM

ABOVE: Inside view of Ochsner and Orcutt Co. Hardware store, 312-314 Nebraska St., Sioux City, 1906. COURTESY PEARL ORCUTT AUSTIN FAMILY

ABOVE RIGHT: Joe Kelley's home and general store, 1315 W. Third St., Sioux City, 1907. Daughters Mable, Mary and Adora are pictured. COURTESY ADORA SCHNEIDERS

RIGHT: Bicycle delivery boys for Western Union Telegraph and Cable, 519 Fifth St., Sioux City, around 1910. COURTESY SIOUX CITY MUSEUM

ABOVE: Exterior view of Ochsner and Orcutt Co. Hardware store, 312-314 Nebraska St., Sioux City, 1906.
COURTESY PEARL ORCUTT AUSTIN FAMILY

LEFT: D.S. Anthony Trunk Factory, 411 Fifth St., Sioux City, around 1910. Mr. Anthony is pictured waiting on a customer.
COURTESY SIOUX CITY MUSEUM

ABOVE: The Little Gem Cafe, 914 Fourth St., Sioux City, 1914. Owners James and Margaret Magirl and Clara and Agnes are pictured. COURTESY SIOUX CITY MUSEUM

ABOVE RIGHT: Fleet of REOs for the Hanford Produce Company, Barish Motor Company, southeast corner of Fifth and Pearl streets, circa 1918. COURTESY SIOUX CITY MUSEUM

RIGHT: Team with wagon being unloaded at a warehouse on Third St., Sioux City, circa 1915. The men are unidentified. COURTESY BILL MCPHERSON

ABOVE: Moore Shenkberg Grocer Company, Third and Pierce streets, Sioux City, about 1916. Photo shows crew standing around a Walker electric delivery truck. COURTESY SIOUX CITY MUSEUM

ABOVE LEFT: H. Harrison Meat Market, Fourth Street, Sioux City, 1912. Owner H. Harrison is pictured in the middle. COURTESY BILL MCPHERSON

LEFT: Customers gather for a sale at the T.S. Martin Department Store, located on Fourth Street, Sioux City, about 1915. The store, one of Sioux City's three big department stores, was founded by T.S. Martin in 1880. COURTESY SIOUX CITY MUSEUM

ABOVE: Sioux City Motor Sales Company, Sioux City, at 317-319 Fifth St., circa 1920. COURTESY SIOUX CITY MUSEUM

ABOVE RIGHT: Tackaberry Grocery warehouse employees, Sioux City, about 1920. The company was a wholesale grocer from 1878 until 1924 and was located at Third and Wall streets. COURTESY SIOUX CITY MUSEUM

RIGHT: Interior view of Carlson's Grocery, 3444 Jones St., Sioux City, 1922. Ester Carlson is pictured on the far left and Merritt Carlson in the long apron on the right. COURTESY JOAN MCDERMOTT

ABOVE: Interior view of Coney Island restaurant with owner George Margeas (far left) and staff, 510 Nebraska St., Sioux City, 1924. COURTESY STEVE MARGEAS

ABOVE LEFT: Ryal Miller Chevrolet dealership at the northeast corner of Fifth and Nebraska streets, Sioux City, 1920s. In the center of the image is Coney Island Hotdogs. COURTESY SIOUX CITY MUSEUM

LEFT: Griffin and Griffin Law Firm, Sioux City, early 1920s. Thomas Griffin, attorney (behind the desk) and Mike Waters (right), a banker. COURTESY SIOUX CITY MUSEUM

ABOVE: The General Tire Company, operated by I.R. McGowan, northwest corner of Ninth and Pierce streets, Sioux City, around 1930.
COURTESY SIOUX CITY MUSEUM

LEFT: Voss Lunch, 711 Fourth St., Sioux City, about 1920s. From left: unidentified, Bill Lee, Marie Mosetter, Clayton Brower, Napoleon Girard, Hobson Blackwell, Fritz Sommermeyer. Standing at right: owner, Bill Voss. The restaurant opened December 1914 and closed 1930. COURTESY CHARLOTTE PAUL

OPPOSITE: Westin's Grocery Store, 411 24th St., Sioux City, 1927. Pictured from left: Olaf Westin, Bill Linn, Bill Cross (butcher) and Emma Linn Westin.
COURTESY LYNNE BOULDEN

ABOVE: The Capitol Laundry with delivery trucks and drivers, 505-507 Pearl St., Sioux City, early 1930s. Owner Syl Cusack is pictured in the straw hat on the right. COURTESY KAY AND BOB COACHER

TOP: Len O'Harrow Shoe Store, Sioux City. COURTESY MARY LOU O'CONNOR SHUCK

RIGHT: Alicia Pettit played the violin on radio in Sioux City, 1930s. She later entertained the troops during World War II. COURTESY LANI PETTIT

OPPOSITE: Harley McPherson (left) and Ed West (right) with a wagon full of feed, circa 1927. Harley McPherson worked for the city street department, and Ed West was a laborer at Armour & Co. COURTESY BILL MCPHERSON

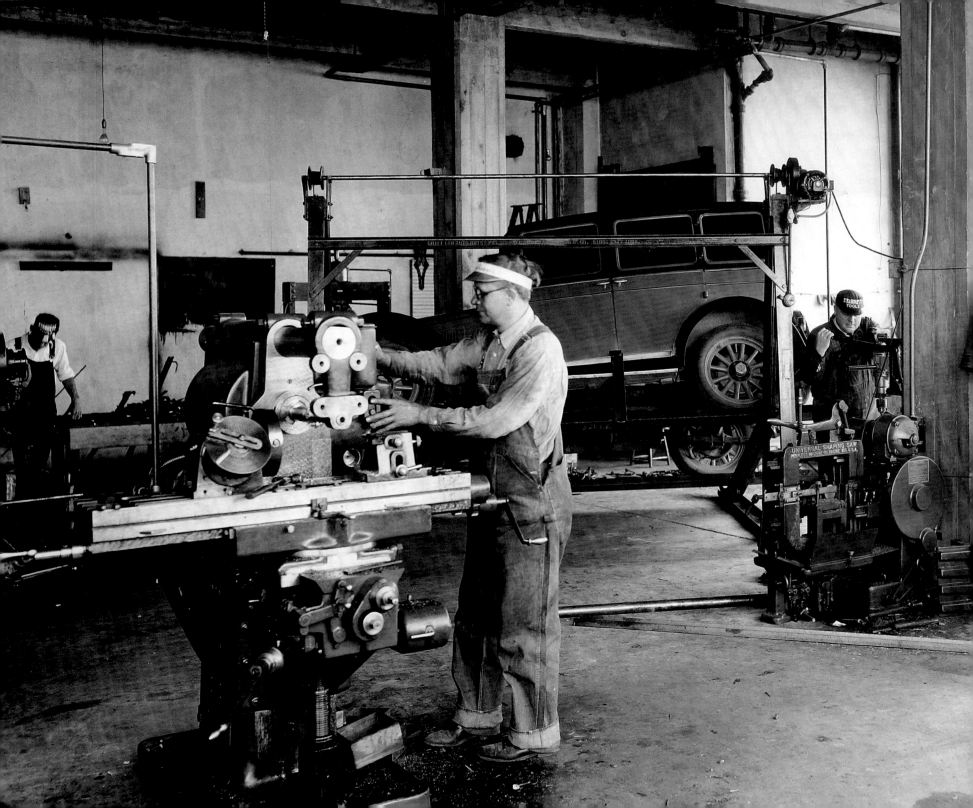

CHAPTER FOUR

AGRICULTURE AND INDUSTRY

When the General Land Office established a Sioux City Land District in 1855, a buying frenzy ensued. Folks out east were eager to get a piece of potential prosperity. As a result, land values rose; homes and stores were quickly constructed. A boom was on.

When eastern banks failed in 1857, that rush collapsed. The land was sold at sheriff's sales or went back to the government. The population, as a result, plummeted.

Sioux City's location, however, couldn't be ignored. Because it was a great distribution point for farmers and the U.S. Army, retailers were able to do business. Hogs became a good "crop" because their meat could be cured and sold elsewhere.

Realizing as much, businessman James E. Booge built a slaughterhouse at Fifth and Water streets in 1866. Today, he's considered the father of Sioux City's meatpacking industry , the one who gave the area an identity and helped it grow. By 1883, there were 13 livestock firms in Sioux City, eager to take advantage of the city's access to eastern markets through rail and water transportation.

In 1884, the Union Stock Yards Company was organized and another boom was beginning to take shape. To handle the influx, hotels and other ancillary businesses began to appear. Booge became a millionaire from his association and sold his plant in 1891 to Union Stock Yards Company. Some say he got out just in time.

In 1892, the Floyd River went on a rampage and, according to the Sioux City Daily Tribune, "the work of years disappeared in an hour." Twenty-five people died, more than 3,000 were left homeless. Nearly every aspect of the industry was damaged. Undaunted, Union Stock Yards officials moved to higher ground and resumed business three days later. By fall, newspapers were talking about the industry's "brilliant future."

The Sioux City story, however, is filled with bouts of disaster – natural or man-made – that threatened to shake its foundation. The meatpacking industry wasn't alone. Others suffered the bruises of economic downfalls only to rebuild and, in some cases, come back stronger.

Other agricultural businesses found a home here, too, and have managed to thrive. Today, it's not uncommon to find countless businesses that have been around for more than 100 years. Tenacity and determination are often the underlying factors.

OPPOSITE: E.A. Arndt Company manufactured many items including the Griffith Automatic Car Hoist (seen in the background), 504 W. Fifth St., Sioux City, 1929. COURTESY SIOUX CITY MUSEUM

ABOVE: Street grading on the 1200 block of Nebraska Street, about 1895. COURTESY SIOUX CITY MUSEUM

ABOVE LEFT: Interior of the Silberhorn Packing Co., the second meat packing plant to locate in the Floyd River bottoms, Sioux City, photo 1890. COURTESY SIOUX CITY MUSEUM

LEFT: This farm is believed to be on Sioux City's north side around 20th and Nebraska streets, about 1890. COURTESY SIOUX CITY MUSEUM

OPPOSITE: Employees of the Sioux City Plow Works, 103 S. Iowa St., Sioux City, 1886. Man standing in the window may be Charles Aronson. COURTESY SIOUX CITY MUSEUM

LEFT: Thuet Bros. "World's Greatest Horse Auction Sale," Sioux City stockyards, 1900. The auction house sold 250 boxcars full of horses in 250 minutes. COURTESY ERIC GEORGESEN

BELOW LEFT: Farmers dropping off milk cans at the Fairmont Creamery Company, Sioux City, 1925. COURTESY SIOUX CITY MUSEUM

OPPOSITE TOP LEFT: Electric streetcars being repaired at the shop located at Second and Water streets, Sioux City, about 1910. COURTESY SIOUX CITY MUSEUM

OPPOSITE TOP RIGHT: Ice collection on the Big Sioux at the old Military Road bridge, Sioux City, 1908. The ice was cut from frozen rivers and stored in the spring and summer for use in home ice-boxes and as well as for industrial uses. COURTESY JOE STABILE

OPPOSITE BOTTOM: This photo shows a Palmer Candy Company packing room in the 209 Douglas St. plant, Sioux City, about 1912. The team members would have been packing chocolates into 5-pound boxes which would then be sold to many retail stores to put out in the candy counters and display jars. COURTESY PALMER CANDY COMPANY

ABOVE: A production area of the Palmer Candy Company making creams, caramels and jell candies, Sioux City. The creams and other candies would be cooked in steam kettles and then deposited into large mold trays. After cooling and setting up for 12 to 24 hours they would be removed to then be covered with chocolate. COURTESY PALMER CANDY COMPANY

LEFT: Robb-Ross Company food manufacturer, Sioux City, 1929. Employees are shown working on the vinegar bottling line. The company was started in 1920. COURTESY SIOUX CITY MUSEUM

OPPOSITE TOP LEFT: Livestock Exchange Building in the stockyards, Sioux City, circa 1920. Charles H. Wright on horse on left. COURTESY SIOUX CITY MUSEUM

OPPOSITE TOP RIGHT: A 32-horsepower steam tractor, Sioux City, about 1910. COURTESY SIOUX CITY MUSEUM

OPPOSITE BOTTOM LEFT: Lewis Dreves, Sioux City, 1920s. Dreves was a boilermaker by trade. COURTESY GRACE CALHOUN KAVANAUGH

OPPOSITE BOTTOM RIGHT: The Sioux Honey Association processing plant, Fourth Street, 1929. COURTESY SIOUX CITY MUSEUM

LEFT: Work in progress at the Sioux City Power Plant, Riverside area of Sioux City, 1931. COURTESY STEVEN KOETTERS

BELOW LEFT: Typical American farm scene, Sioux City, 1935. From left: Grant Holbrook Sr. (manager); daughters Marjorie and Mary Jane; Mervin McQuillen, hired-hand; and son Grant Holbrook Jr. With this team of six Percheron horses and equipment, Mr. Holbrook and his crew worked Doughtery Farm, 260 acres on 28th Street (across from Holiday Village). The horses names are: Queen, Jenny, Bud, Prince, Billy and Pet. COURTESY MOEINE C. BLAKER

OPPOSITE TOP LEFT: Laurel and Hardy in a promotional photo for Kari-Keen Karrier, Sioux City, 1930. The locally made box provided external storage for cars that otherwise did not have trunks. COURTESY SIOUX CITY MUSEUM

OPPOSITE BOTTOM LEFT: Sioux City Journal "old-timers" gather for a reunion photo, 1930. From left: E.P. Heizer, W.R. Perkins, A.F. Allen, Paul Caldwell, W.H. Sammons, Sam McCullough, E.H. Brown, Fred Davis, John W. Carey, Henry Cody, Paul C. Howe and Dean Wheeler. COURTESY SIOUX CITY MUSEUM

OPPOSITE RIGHT: Unidentified youth with three hogs at the Inter-State Livestock Fair in Woodland Park, south of Riverside, prior to 1926. This was probably a 4-H project. COURTESY JOE STABILE

BELOW: A.F. Allen, editor of the Sioux City Journal, 1939. COURTESY SIOUX CITY MUSEUM

CHAPTER FIVE

EDUCATION

Sober faces stare out from posed pictures. But they hardly tell the story of schools in the early days of Sioux City.

Eager to educate their children, early civic leaders invited teachers to join their adventure. A building, however, hadn't been constructed to house them.

In 1857, the first – Mary E. Wilkins – ventured to Sioux City by riverboat and was surprised to discover "there were no books but there were a lot of children, bright and anxious to learn." The schoolhouse, she told The Sioux City Journal, "which was to be finished by May 1, was not nearly completed." Nevertheless, she moved in to the building at 710 Nebraska St. and the work began. By 1859, three schools had opened; by 1869 the district was formally organized.

A cornerstone for what was then called "Central School" was laid July 1, 1869. The building was constructed for $25,000 and was later named Hunt School in honor of the first president of the board of education, A. M. Hunt. Today, another school with the same name is still in operation.

With growth in full force, Sioux City continued its building spree and annexed several townships. Eleven schools were built between 1885 and 1890. On May 23, 1893, officials dedicated Sioux City High School. In September, with 290 pupils and nine teachers, it opened. Some called it "the palace." Others referred to it as "The Castle on the Hill," a name which stuck even after it was dubbed Central High School.

In 1928, Marianist Brothers began Trinity High School as a place to educate Catholic boys.

Higher education wasn't overlooked, either. Morningside College was founded as a four-year co-educational liberal arts institution in 1894; Trinity College was established in 1913 as a four-year Catholic educational institution; Briar Cliff College followed in 1930.

Wilkins, you might say, got it right. The youth of the region were definitely anxious to learn.

OPPOSITE: Students and teachers, Sioux City, 1929. Helen McCoy McIntyre is in the third row from left, second desk from front (with bangs and dark blouse).
COURTESY MARILYN MCINTYRE CHADWICK

ABOVE: Sherwin Land Office, Sioux City, 1880. The building was multi-purpose also used by the First Congregational Church and Eastside Primary School during the 1860s and 1870s. COURTESY SIOUX CITY MUSEUM

ABOVE RIGHT: Armstrong Grammar School, Sioux City, about 1892. The school started in 1882 and closed in 1925 and provided secondary education (sixth grade and up). It was located at the southeast corner of Eighth and Pierce streets. COURTESY SIOUX CITY MUSEUM

RIGHT: Everett School class photo, W. Third and Rebecca streets, Sioux City, about 1905. The school was built in 1888. COURTESY SIOUX CITY MUSEUM

ABOVE: Irving Elementary School students during exercises, Sioux City, 1890s. The school was located on the southeast corner of 11th and Jennings streets. COURTESY SIOUX CITY MUSEUM

ABOVE: Webster Elementary School, W. Fifth and Market streets, Sioux City, 1890s. COURTESY SIOUX CITY MUSEUM

ABOVE RIGHT: Bancroft School class photo, Sioux City, late 1890s. The school, named for historian George Bancroft, opened in 1888, and was located at 11th and Pearl streets. COURTESY SIOUX CITY MUSEUM

RIGHT: East Third Street School class photo, Sioux City, about 1890s. The elementary school was located at Third and Chambers streets at this time. It was moved in 1906. COURTESY SIOUX CITY MUSEUM

ABOVE: The graduating class of the Sioux City Normal training class, 1894. Those pictured: Miss Conlan, Mattie Fister, Ernestine Corkery, Mattie Adair, Mrs. Furgeson, Ruth Weitz, Miss Brown, Elizabeth Rood, Mattie Shoup and Stella Baker. COURTESY SIOUX CITY MUSEUM

ABOVE LEFT: The College of Medicine football team, Sioux City, 1899. The college was a short-lived school in the early 20th century and was located in the YMCA building at Seventh and Pierce streets. William Jepson was one of the founding members of the College of Medicine, he also helped start the Samaritan Hospital, a predecessor of Unity Point. COURTESY SIOUX CITY MUSEUM

ABOVE MIDDLE : The College of Medicine, Sioux City, about 1905. COURTESY SIOUX CITY MUSEUM

LEFT: Dwight Elementary School class photo, Seventh and Wall streets, Sioux City, about 1907. COURTESY SIOUX CITY MUSEUM

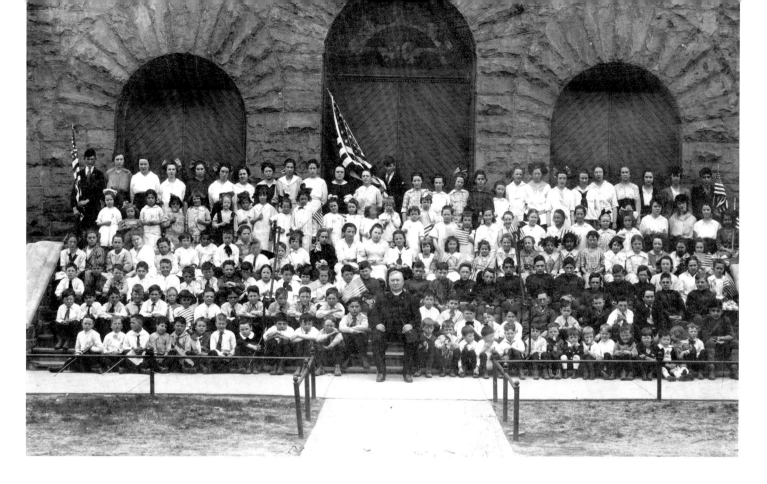

LEFT: Eighth grade graduation class, St. Joseph school, St. Joseph Catholic Church, Sioux City, 1911. Emily Hayes Betz is pictured second from the left in the second row.
COURTESY BARBARA (BETZ) SWANSON

BELOW LEFT: The boiler room of Sioux City High School, about 1912. This was the city's main high school from 1892 to 1972. The school was located at 12th and Jackson streets.
COURTESY SIOUX CITY MUSEUM

BELOW RIGHT: South Bottoms School class photo, Sioux City, circa 1915.
COURTESY KEVIN BETZ

OPPOSITE: Sioux City High School baseball team, about 1915. COURTESY SIOUX CITY MUSEUM

ABOVE: Charismatic Sioux City School Superintendent Melvin Green Clark is surrounded by family members in this Clark family photo, 1925. Seated from left: Luella Clark (sister), Lamira Clark (mother), George Thorpe Clark and Dorothy June Clark. Back row, from left: Harry Clark (son) and Lola, "Colleen" Maude Clark (wife), Melvin Green Clark, Robert Clark (son), Wilson Clark (son) and Wilson's wife Mae Thorpe Clark. The dog is Prince.
COURTESY KAREN AND RUSTY CLARK

ABOVE RIGHT: Three thousand Junior High School students gather at Gilman Park to participate in group exercises, 17th and Omaha streets, Sioux City, 1927.
COURTESY SIOUX CITY MUSEUM

RIGHT: The ground breaking of Briar Cliff College, Heelan Hall, 1929. The cornerstone was set on March 30th, 1930. The Most Rev. Edmond Heelan, Bishop of the Sioux City Diocese (far right). COURTESY BRIAR CLIFF UNIVERSITY

LEFT: Trinity High School cheerleaders, Sioux City, 1933-34. COURTESY JANET FLANAGAN

FAR LEFT: Trinity High School's football captain Orville Fortin, shakes hands with opposing team captain Bill Burns before a game, Sioux City, about 1934. COURTESY JANET FLANAGAN

BELOW: Trinity High School's Joe Gantz is pictured here with the ball in a game against a team from Akron, Iowa, 1933. Gantz would later own and operate Joe Gantz Steakhouse for several decades in Sioux City. COURTESY JANET FLANAGAN

ABOVE LEFT: Miss Bliss' second grade class at Bryant School, Sioux City, 1936. Pictured in back row, ninth from left, is Carol Anderson, granddaughter of Andrew G. Anderson, 1892 flood hero. Also pictured, in front row, fifth from left, is Earle Grueskin, future Sioux City mayor. COURTESY CAROL ANDERSON FERGUSON

ABOVE RIGHT: Trinity High School basketball squad, Sioux City, 1935-36. Front row, from left: Alex Yokunaitis, Phil Donohue, Orvie Fortin and Bud Bets. Back row, from left: Coach Don Joynt, Paul Frank, Don Martin, Bob Kelley, Max Braunger and Ray Murphy. COURTESY JANET FLANAGAN

LEFT: Baccalaureate procession with high school and college students and faculty, Trinity High School, Sioux City, 1935. COURTESY JANET FLANAGAN

OPPOSITE: In 1929, only briar patches covered a 175-foot hill located on the western outskirts of Sioux City, Iowa. But two people – Mother Mary Dominica Wieneke, Major Superior of the Sisters of Saint Francis, and the Most Reverend Edmond Heelan, Bishop of the Sioux City Diocese –had a dream. They saw that hill crowned with a Catholic college for women. Mother Dominica and Bishop Heelan met on March 9, 1929, with members of the Sioux City community who committed themselves to raising $25,000 to support the establishment of the college in Sioux City. After this showing of community support, significant events followed in rapid succession. On Sept. 18, 1930, the college, named Briar Cliff after the hill on which it is located, was dedicated. Four days later, 25 women started classes in Heelan Hall, the only building on campus. COURTESY BRIAR CLIFF UNIVERSITY

ABOVE: Riverview School faculty, Sioux City, 1938. Esther Coacher is on the far right. She taught at the school for about 30 years.
COURTESY KAY AND BOB COACHER

ABOVE RIGHT: Trinity High School basketball team as they prepare to leave for the state Catholic Basketball Tournament in Dubuque, Iowa, 1935.
COURTESY JANET FLANAGAN

RIGHT: West Junior High band, Sioux City, 1924.
COURTESY SIOUX CITY MUSEUM

OPPOSITE: Sixth-grade class photo, McKinley School, Sioux City, 1939.
COURTESY KEVIN BETZ

CHAPTER SIX

COMMUNITY

What drives a community? Schools, for one. Religion for another.

Soon after Sioux City was surveyed between 1854 and 1855, the Rev. Charles D. Martin arrived, hoping to share the gospel. The Rev. Thomas M. Chestnut came a few months later, hoping to build a church. Using space in what buildings existed, both preached until the weather made services difficult. They both left for homes in Illinois and, in the spring of 1857, Chestnut returned with his wife.

Martin launched the Methodist Episcopal Church; Chestnut established the Presbyterian Church. While both tried to finish the city's first church building, they were often hampered by the ability to raise funds. Both had plans, but the Presbyterians had the edge. In a charitable move, Methodists decided to join their fellow Christians to get a building finished. In the Sept. 3, 1859, Sioux City Journal, they announced that the building had been completed. Religion had planted roots in the region.

In short order, Congregationalists, Baptists, Episcopalians, Roman Catholics and Lutherans followed. Social activities sprang from the churches; residents desired more to occupy their free time.

On Jan. 14, 1871, the Academy of Music, was dedicated. Located on the south side of Fourth Street, it was three stories tall, seated 800 and featured state-of-the-art stage equipment. Actor Selden Irwin brought his acting company for the opening. He called the hall "one of the finest west of Chicago" and, quickly, it became a community center hosting everything from political rallies to, yes, church services. An opera house became the next goal for residents. The cornerstone was placed during the 1887 Corn Palace Festival and the building was named in honor of Frank H. Peavey, a businessman.

The Peavey Grand Opera House opened in 1888, prompting The Journal to rave: "It is the literal and absolute truth to say that in the United States there is no city the size of Sioux City which has so beautiful and perfect a theater." Edwin Booth, Sarah Bernhardt, Maude Adams and some of the most acclaimed shows from New York stopped at the Peavey.

The stage was set for other advancements in the arts, sports and, of course, religion.

OPPOSITE: Girl Scouts at Stone Park ready to take a dive into the swimming pool, Sioux City, about 1920. COURTESY SIOUX CITY MUSEUM

ABOVE: Placement of the cornerstone for St. Thomas Episcopal Church, 12th and Douglas streets, Sioux City, Aug. 12, 1891. The church is still standing. COURTESY SIOUX CITY MUSEUM

TOP LEFT: Clara Latham, Sioux City, about 1890. She and her family had a park built on their land and subsequently set up a trust fund to maintain them. Today it is the Latham Memorial Park in Sioux City. COURTESY SIOUX CITY MUSEUM

TOP RIGHT: This interior view of the 1889 Sioux City Corn Palace shows the Perkins Bros. Company booth. After the exhibit was over, all the grains, corn, etc. were auctioned off to local farmers. Even the wood sub-structure was sold. COURTESY SIOUX CITY MUSEUM

RIGHT: Johann Hacker and wife Fran Ziska Franz Hacker, Sioux City, about 1866. The couple were partners with the Huerth family running one of the brickyards in the Greenville area. They had five children. COURTESY DELORES SOULE

ABOVE: Construction crew for St. Thomas Episcopal Church take a break and pose for the camera, Sioux City, about 1891. COURTESY SIOUX CITY MUSEUM

RIGHT: Dedication of St. Joseph Catholic Church, Eighth and Iowa streets, Sioux City, Sept. 3, 1899.
COURTESY BARBARA (BETZ) SWANSON

BELOW LEFT: Malone African-American Methodist Church, at 513 Main St., Sioux City, about 1900. This building is the oldest church still being used by its original congregation — 1887 to present.
COURTESY SIOUX CITY MUSEUM

BELOW RIGHT: Lilian Mousseau (White), Sioux City, about 1900. Lilian was active in social service and also an accomplished musician, performer and music publisher.
COURTESY SIOUX CITY MUSEUM

ABOVE: Class photo of St. Paul's Lutheran Church school, grades one through eight, Codfish Hill (Seventh and Jackson streets), Sioux City, 1898. COURTESY ST. PAUL'S LUTHERAN CHURCH/BERNIE ATTEMA

LEFT: Charles L. Peck (left) and his uncle Floyd Peck pose for this studio portrait, Sioux City, 1898. COURTESY L. JUNE YOUNG

RIGHT: Sisters Jenny, Tilly, Rose and Mary Schlupp gather around what is now a family heirloom table, 914 Douglas St., Sioux City, 1904.
COURTESY CAROL BIRMINGHAM STRAIT

BELOW RIGHT: Lewis Dreves, Sioux City, 1903. Lewis married Ida Loetz and was a boilermaker by trade. As a hobby, he made violins.
COURTESY GRACE CALHOUN KAVANAUGH

BELOW: Hawkeye Club members in front of the club at Eighth and Douglas streets, Sioux City, about 1905. Members are shown during what may be a possible initiation ceremony. The club was a businessman's social club.
COURTESY SIOUX CITY MUSEUM

ABOVE: St. Joseph Catholic Church, Eighth and Iowa streets, Sioux City, early 1900s. COURTESY BARBARA (BETZ) SWANSON

ABOVE LEFT: Burns family photo, Sioux City, 1902. Pictured from left: Josie, William and daughter Elizabeth. COURTESY ELIZABETH EVERIST

LEFT: First Baptist Church, northeast corner of Fifth and Nebraska streets, 1908. The church was built in 1882. COURTESY SIOUX CITY MUSEUM

ABOVE: Members of the Inter Ocean Cycle Club, Sioux City, about 1900. COURTESY SIOUX CITY MUSEUM

ABOVE: Banquet at the Riverside Boat Club, along the Big Sioux River near Riverside Park, Sioux City, around 1910. Sioux City's five boat clubs played an important role in summer time social activities at the turn of the century. COURTESY SIOUX CITY MUSEUM

LEFT: Chester Maran is pictured holding baby sister Mary with his other siblings, Veda and Ed, at his side, Sioux City, 1904. COURTESY ELIZABETH EVERIST

ABOVE: Mt. Zion Baptist Church congregation, W. Sixth and Bluff streets, Sioux City, about 1915.
COURTESY SIOUX CITY MUSEUM

RIGHT: Mary Maran and brother Edward are dressed up for winter, Sioux City, 1907. COURTESY ELIZABETH EVERIST

LEFT : Family photo of Marie Dreves (Bauer) (left), Catherine Dreves (Calhoun) and brother Leo, Sioux City, 1913. Leo died of polio at age 7. COURTESY GRACE CALHOUN KAVANAUGH

FAR LEFT: Siblings Albert and Genevieve Peck, Sioux City, 1912. COURTESY ELIZABETH EVERIST

BELOW LEFT: Sarah Jane Franklin Herman Bristow (center in back) and her five daughters, 18th and Center streets, Sioux City, 1915. Daughters are, from left: Elisabeth, Louise, Iona Vivian, Florence and Lavern. The youngest of eight, Iona "Viv" graduated from Central in 1925. She was in the first class from Smith School to go to West Junior High. COURTESY DELORES SOULE

RIGHT: Frank Allen Pettit Sr. and Frank Allan Pettit Jr., Sioux City, 1912. COURTESY LANI PETTIT

OPPOSITE: Sioux City Chamber of Commerce banquet at the Commerce Building, Sixth and Nebraska streets, circa 1917. COURTESY SIOUX CITY MUSEUM

BELOW: Bert Olaf Anderson, courting his future wife Esther Caroline Anderson (daughter of Andrew G. Anderson, 1892 flood hero) before their 1916 marriage. Photo was taken in front of 1112 10th St., Sioux City, where she lived for a short time with her widowed mother, Margaret DeSmet Anderson. (Note: Both Esther's maiden and married surnames were Anderson.) COURTESY CAROL ANDERSON FERGUSON

RIGHT: Rosina Marie Hacker, Sioux City, about 1914. She married Lawrence McQuirk, a conductor for the Northern Railroad, that same year and together they lived in a house next to the Greenville Drugstore their entire lives. The couple had six daughters and one son. COURTESY DELORES SOULE

FAR RIGHT: Esther Savary and Merritt Carlson, Sioux City, 1918. The Merritts were owners of Carlson's Grocery. COURTESY JOAN MCDERMOTT

BELOW RIGHT: Bernard Coyne shown here with a player from the Sioux City Packers and a player from an unidentified Denver team, Sioux City, 1917. Born in rural Oto, Iowa, Bernard was 8-foot-2 inches and weighed more than 400 pounds. COURTESY JOE STABILE

OPPOSITE TOP LEFT: Harold Edwards and Mayme Edwards (mother and son) sitting on the running board of the family's Model T, 2508 First St., Sioux City, about 1920. COURTESY VICKIE (EDWARDS) HENRICHSEN

OPPOSITE TOP RIGHT: Margaret, Warren, Robert and Howard McIntyre, 3110 Jones St., Sioux City, circa 1923. COURTESY MARILYN MCINTYRE CHADWICK

OPPOSITE BOTTOM: Catholic Cadet Corps band, Sioux City, about 1920. COURTESY SIOUX CITY MUSEUM

LEFT: Girl Scouts at Stone Park enjoying a swim, Sioux City, about 1920. COURTESY SIOUX CITY MUSEUM

OPPOSITE: Girl Scout encampment at Stone Park, Sioux City, about 1920. COURTESY SIOUX CITY MUSEUM

BELOW LEFT: Girl Scouts at Stone Park, preparing for a foot race, Sioux City, about 1920. COURTESY SIOUX CITY MUSEUM

ABOVE: Two-year-old Carol Anderson with her doll buggy, Sioux City, 1931. Carol is the granddaughter of Andrew G. Anderson, 1892 flood hero. Photo taken by her mother Esther Anderson in Sioux City.
COURTESY CAROL ANDERSON FERGUSON

ABOVE RIGHT: Mary Schupp in front of her home at 914 Douglas St., Sioux City, 1923. COURTESY CAROL BIRMINGHAM STRAIT

RIGHT: Anna Carlson (wife), Merritt (son), Rudy (son) and Edward Carlson (father) on their way to church at Augustana Lutheran in Sioux City, 1918.
COURTESY JOAN MCDERMOTT

ABOVE: Local aviator Floyd Cox, is shown here in his flight suit, Sioux City, about 1930. Cox held many air speed records. He was killed in a plane crash 1931. COURTESY SIOUX CITY MUSEUM

LEFT: Raymond James Mahr Jr. on a pedal car, Sioux City, 1922. He later went on to become the first Sioux City Fire Marshall of Fire Prevention. COURTESY JERRY MAHR

ABOVE: Clara Mosetter and Marguerite Mosetter on the streets of Sioux City, 1928. Both worked in the Sioux City theaters (Hipp, Victory, Capitol) for many years.
COURTESY CHARLOTTE PAUL

ABOVE MIDDLE: Mildred (Mert) Birmingham at her family home, 2823 Pierce St., Sioux City, 1926.
COURTESY CAROL BIRMINGHAM STRAIT

ABOVE RIGHT: George and Pat Rowe sitting on top of dredging equipment, McCook Lake, 1931. COURTESY PATRICIA LAMOUREUX

BELOW RIGHT: Hazel Erskine with sons Vernon and Maxwell, Morningside, Sioux City, 1929. COURTESY MAC ERSKINE

ABOVE: Catherine Dreves Calhoun pictured outside her home on E. Eighth Street, Sioux City, 1928. She completed eighth grade and worked at Pelletier's as a cashier. COURTESY GRACE CALHOUN KAVANAUGH

LEFT: The Sample family, Sioux City, 1929. Leon "Dewey" Sample Sr., wife Alma and son Leon "Dewey" Sample Jr. COURTESY DEBI HEATON

ABOVE LEFT: Philip Ofstehage and his uncle Fred Dahl on a visit to Sioux City for supplies, 1938. Together they farmed northwest of Elk Point, S.D. COURTESY BERNARD AND GLENDA OFSTEHAGE

ABOVE MIDDLE: Five kids and a goat, West 23rd and Everett, Sioux City, 1932. From left: Archie Peck, Roger Peck, Loren Peck, Harold Butler and baby Monte Asbra on Harold's pet goat. COURTESY L. JUNE YOUNG

ABOVE RIGHT: Siblings sitting on the running board of the family's new 1932 Buick, W. 23rd and Everett streets, Sioux City, 1932. From left: June, Norma, Loren, Roger and Archie Peck. COURTESY L. JUNE YOUNG

RIGHT: Trinity High School band, Sioux City, 1930s. COURTESY JANET FLANAGAN

LEFT: Brothers Bill, Richard and Bob Betz posing for their picture, Sioux City, 1930. Richard is sitting on the tricycle. COURTESY BARBARA (BETZ) SWANSON

FAR LEFT: Josie Burns, daughter Elizabeth Everist, son William Hagan and daughter Betty Hagan Everist represent four generations, Sioux City, about 1935. COURTESY ELIZABETH EVERIST

BELOW: Pearl Orcutt Oschner, daughter of W.W. Orcutt, founder of Orcutt Hardware, Sioux City, about 1939. COURTESY PEARL ORCUTT AUSTIN FAMILY

CHAPTER SEVEN

PUBLIC SERVICE

Bridges. Schools. Theaters. Churches. Government buildings.
They didn't spring up by accident. They were fostered by citizens who wanted to see their community improve, prosper and change.

The 1887 Corn Palace – hailed around the world – proved big things could happen. Businessmen were buoyed by the success. But they also faced an economic depression, floods and fires that threatened to end Sioux City's boom.

In subsequent years, Sioux City's story became one of building. And rebuilding.

Prosperity – in the face of all odds – happened because those civic leaders were determined. They took risks and, in some cases, reaped rewards.

The Sioux City Journal championed various community projects in those building years but didn't cower from questioning their funding. Even in the money-parched Depression years, it urged residents to keep a watchful eye on civic leaders.

Architecture became a focus at the turn of the century and when Woodbury County voters approved a new court house in 1914, some were shocked – The Journal included – that the Board of Supervisors would approve such a radical design.

The architects were William M. Steele and George Elmslie. The building, a tribute to style and function.

Time, then, becomes another factor when gauging value. Given enough time, even the most unlikely concept can seem brilliant.

OPPOSITE: Special police force at the Interstate Fair, Sioux City, 1911. COURTESY SIOUX CITY MUSEUM

RIGHT: Interior view of Fire Station No. 4, Sioux City, about 1895.
COURTESY SIOUX CITY MUSEUM

BELOW LEFT: Dr. William Remsen Smith, a pioneer Sioux City physician, about 1890. Smith moved to Sioux City in 1856 where he practiced medicine for 11 years. In 1863 he was elected mayor of Sioux City. He donated his home to be made into a school which bore his name. The school was torn down in 2011. Two streets, Remsen and Osborne, are named for him and his wife.
COURTESY SIOUX CITY MUSEUM

BELOW RIGHT: Mother Mary Gertrude, 1905. She headed the Benedictine Sisters of Sioux City. She also helped establish St. Monica's Home for Babies and St. Vincent's Hospital. She ran the hospital from 1918 until her death on Sept. 21, 1940.
COURTESY SIOUX CITY MUSEUM

OPPOSITE: Old Hose Company No. 1, 408 Water St., Sioux City, about 1900. COURTESY SIOUX CITY MUSEUM

RIGHT: Sioux City Police Captain Jack Howell, 1909. COURTESY SIOUX CITY MUSEUM

FAR RIGHT: Harry Colvin in Sioux City Police dress uniform, 1908. COURTESY CRAIG CLARK

BELOW: The Sioux City jail, early 1900s. COURTESY SIOUX CITY MUSEUM

ABOVE: Sioux City police checking a suspect, Sioux City Police Department, early 1900s. COURTESY SIOUX CITY MUSEUM

ABOVE LEFT: Police or federal agents with confiscated liquor, Sioux City, about 1920. COURTESY SIOUX CITY MUSEUM

LEFT: Men and equipment comprising the No. 3 Engine Company at 515 Iowa St., Sioux City, 1920. This photo includes the No. 3 truck, "Pumping Billy" and No. 3 engine. COURTESY SIOUX CITY MUSEUM

ABOVE: World War I recruit training at Sioux City High School, Sioux City, 1918. COURTESY SIOUX CITY MUSEUM

OPPOSITE: Recruits were receiving training in semaphore and radio field station operation, Sioux City, 1918. COURTESY SIOUX CITY MUSEUM

RIGHT: The No. 5 Hose Company, Sioux City Fire Department, 1926. The station was located in the stockyards. COURTESY MAC ERSKINE

BELOW RIGHT: Sioux City motorcycle police, about 1920. Earl Morgan is on the left, the other officer is unidentified. COURTESY SIOUX CITY MUSEUM

BELOW: Engine Company No. 3, 515 Iowa St., Sioux City, 1920. COURTESY SIOUX CITY MUSEUM

ABOVE: Fire Station No. 1, 515 Water St., Sioux City, 1929. COURTESY SIOUX CITY MUSEUM

LEFT: Fire Station No. 4, 14th and Nebraska streets, Sioux City, 1929. COURTESY SIOUX CITY MUSEUM

FAR LEFT: Sioux City Police Chief Ray Mahr Jr., 1938. COURTESY JERRY MAHR

CHAPTER EIGHT

RECREATION AND CELEBRATION

Even though they're buzz words for employers today, "quality of life" was important to Sioux Cityans, even in the very beginning.

That's evidenced by the construction of five corn palaces, several theaters, dance pavilions, skating rinks, ball parks, a speedway and, in 1935, a music pavilion.

In 1906, a park commission bought 30 acres of land on the city's north side. Grass and trees were planted; flower gardens started to emerge. At the dedication in August 1908, a band performed and planted yet another seed. "Fully 3,500 people gathered last night at Grand View Park (and) listened to delightful music," The Journal reported.

Bands continued to play there until the Monahan Post

Band, under the leadership of Leo Kucinski, began a campaign to construct a music shell in Grandview Park. Funds were sought, a design was approved and, thanks to the creation of the Civil Works Administration, the project was a go. A band pavilion became CWA Project No. 217.

Dedicated May 26, 1935, it became home to the Monahan Post Band, which played there every summer until 1948 when it became the Sioux City Municipal Band.

Today, the Municipal Band still performs there, a tribute to the dreamers and do-ers who were able to recognize what draws people to a community. Work? Yes. Opportunity? Of course.

But, for many, it's those three words: Quality of life.

OPPOSITE: Soap Box Derby competitors, downtown Sioux City, 1938. Preliminary heat winner Mel Fox (driver) with Eugene Fox (pusher) shown in car No. 37 (lower right hand corner). The team and car was sponsored by Rains Garage. COURTESY MARILYN FOX

ABOVE: Corn Palace, northwest corner of Fifth and Jackson streets, Sioux City, 1887.
COURTESY SIOUX CITY MUSEUM

RIGHT: Elaborate interior of the 1890 Corn Palace, Sioux City. After the exhibit was over, all the grains, corn, etc. were auctioned to local farmers. Even the wood sub-structure was sold. COURTESY JOE STABILE

ABOVE: Tennis Club players, near Riverside Park, circa 1895.
COURTESY SIOUX CITY MUSEUM

ABOVE LEFT: Team photo of the Sioux City Corn Huskers, most likely at Riverside Park. Sioux City, 1891.
COURTESY SIOUX CITY MUSEUM

LEFT: Pre-game activities at Evans Driving Park, home of the Sioux City Corn Huskers, Sioux City, about 1891. The park was located at 23rd and Center streets.
COURTESY SIOUX CITY MUSEUM

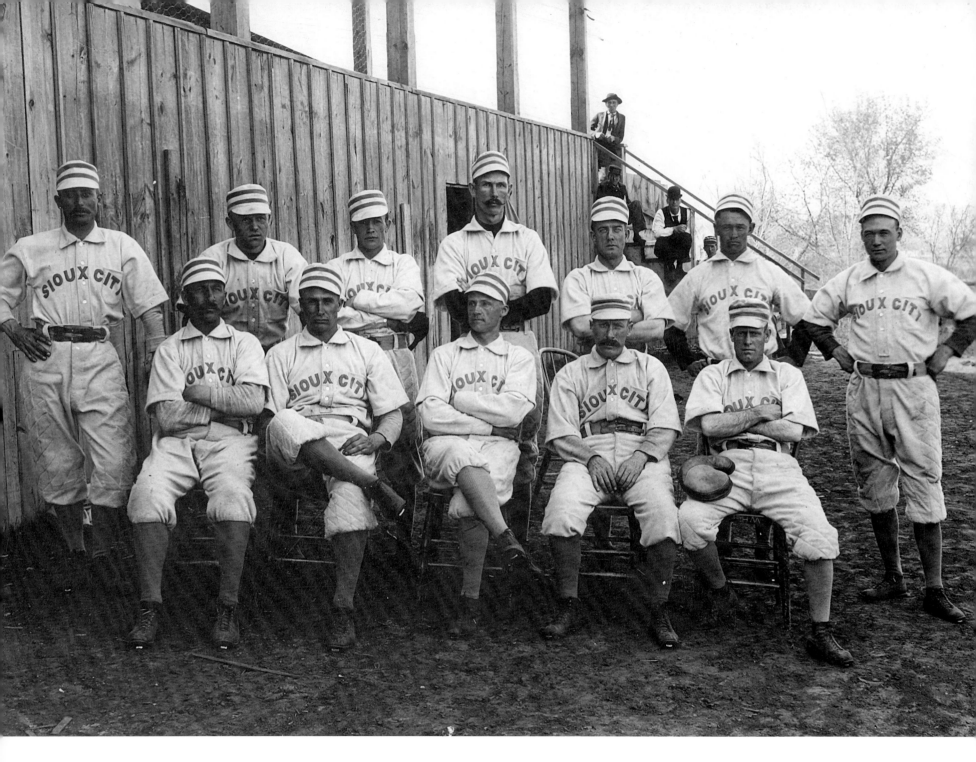

LEFT: Members of the Hagen and Schlupp families gather for dinner at the Washington House Hotel, 510 Pearl St., Sioux City, late 1800s. COURTESY CAROL BIRMINGHAM STRAIT

OPPOSITE: Sioux City Corn Huskers, probably taken at Evans Driving Park Stadium, Sioux City, 1894. COURTESY SIOUX CITY MUSEUM

BELOW LEFT: Sioux City Mondamin Carnival parade entry from W.H. Beck Jeweler, downtown Sioux City, 1900. COURTESY SIOUX CITY MUSEUM

BELOW: Sioux City Carnival parade entry, 1900. COURTESY SIOUX CITY MUSEUM

ABOVE: Wedding photo of Margaret B. Hagman and Charles L. Peck, Whitfield Methodist Church, Sioux City, 1909. COURTESY L. JUNE YOUNG

ABOVE RIGHT: Officers of the Farmer's Loan and Trust Company and their families gather at the Riverside Boat Club, Sioux City, 1903. Sioux City's five boat clubs played an important role in summer time social activities at the turn of the century. COURTESY SIOUX CITY MUSEUM

RIGHT: Fire department contest, held at the Inter-State Fair Grounds, Sioux City, about 1910. COURTESY SIOUX CITY MUSEUM

ABOVE: The steamboat Minnehaha led excursions from Riverside Park off the Big Sioux River, Sioux City, around 1900. COURTESY SIOUX CITY MUSEUM

LEFT: Outfield view of the Sioux City Packers, Riverside Park. Sioux City, circa 1910.
COURTESY SIOUX CITY MUSEUM

OPPOSITE: Sioux City Packers playing at Mizzou Park (where the downtown Tyson Events Center is currently located), Sioux City, about 1910.
COURTESY JOE STABILE

BELOW LEFT: Fans watch the start of a race from under tents at Sioux City Speedway, circa 1912. Grandstands were added in 1914.
COURTESY SIOUX CITY MUSEUM

BELOW: Sioux City Boat Club members on the Big Sioux River behind the Sioux City Boat Club, about 1910. Sioux City's five boat clubs played an important role in summer time social activities at the turn of the century. COURTESY SIOUX CITY MUSEUM

RIGHT: Children getting ready to walk in a parade in Sioux City, about 1916. Iona Vivian Bristow is in white on the left with a bow in back of her hair. She was the youngest of eight children.
COURTESY DELORES SOULE

BELOW RIGHT: Spencer family photo on the occasion of Evalyn Spencer graduating from Central High School, Sioux City, 1918. Standing from left to right: Hazel, Pearl, Charles, Herbert, Earl, Ella and Evalyn. COURTESY DELORES SOULE

BELOW: Crowd gathers for the arrival of the Ringling Brother's Circus at the rail yards near Eighth and Clark streets, Sioux City, circa 1915.
COURTESY SIOUX CITY MUSEUM

ABOVE: Schneiders brothers, Joe, Tony and Victor playing marbles, Sioux City, 1914. COURTESY ADORA SCHNEIDERS

LEFT: Herbert Luke Spencer, Sioux City, 1923. Herbert also played baseball and football and is in the Iowa State Baseball Hall of Fame. Later, when he was older, he umpired for teams in Sioux City. COURTESY DELORES SOULE

FAR LEFT: Wedding day photo of Leon "Dewey" Sample and Alma Sundquist, Sioux City, 1921. COURTESY DEBI HEATON

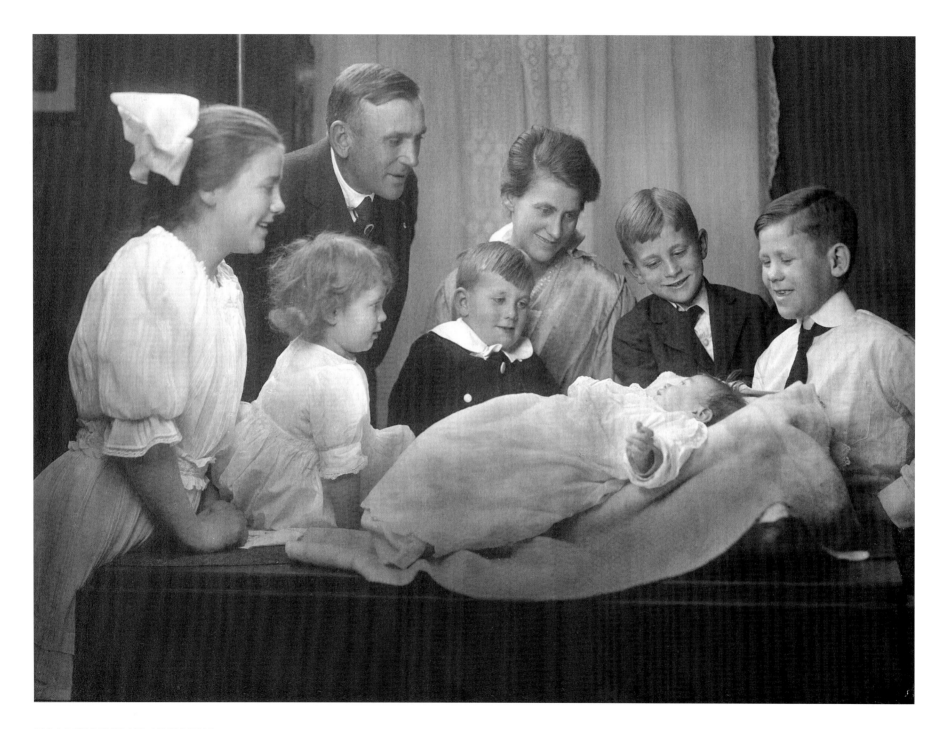

ABOVE: Babe Ruth, Edward Birmingham and Lou Gehrig at an exhibition game at the stockyards in Sioux City, COURTESY CAROL BIRMINGHAM STRAIT

OPPOSITE: Mr. and Mrs. Edward H. Birmingham and children Mert, Louise, Ed, Melvin, Bill and baby Franny, in their home at 2923 Pierce St., Sioux City, about 1918. COURTESY CAROL BIRMINGHAM STRAIT

RIGHT: Esther Coacher cross-county skiing on McKinley Street in Riverside near her home at 921 Edgewater Ave., late 1920s. COURTESY KAY AND BOB COACHER

FAR RIGHT: Jim Bauer and Bill Kartcher in a calf-drawn cart on the occasion of a parade held for Charles Lindbergh, Sioux City, 1927. COURTESY DOUG LEHMAN

BELOW RIGHT: Sunday get-together to enjoy food and family, 1815 Iowa St., Sioux City, 1927. Front row: Leon "Dewey" Sample Jr. and Darline Sturdevant. Back row, from left: Rose Briles Sample, Margaret, Larry Sample, Leona Sturlevant, Alma, Leon "Dewey" Sample Sr. and Harley Sturlevant. COURTESY DEBI HEATON

OPPOSITE: The KSCJ Breakfast Club broadcast with Walter Blaufuss, Don McNeill, Evelyn Lynne and Jack Baker, Sioux City, 1929. COURTESY SIOUX CITY MUSEUM

ABOVE: Chamber of Commerce boosters committee, in front of the Warnock Building, Sioux City, 1929. From left: Raymond C. Cook, Thomas B. Huff, Nittert Aalfs, Cecil H. Mayers, Guy M. Churchill and Ed R. Long. COURTESY SIOUX CITY MUSEUM

RIGHT: The Pettit "family orchestra," Sioux City, circa 1930. From left: Frank "Al" Allan Pettit Jr., Alicia Pettit (Wood), John R. Pettit and Annis Pettit (Cooke). COURTESY LANI PETTIT

FAR RIGHT: George and Pat Rowe next to a horse at 2805 Rebecca St., Sioux City, 1930. The property had a horse stable in back. COURTESY PATRICIA LAMOUREUX

LEFT: Joe Schneiders Jr., with his new Christmas tricycle, 1203 W. Second St., Sioux City, 1931. COURTESY ADORA SCHNEIDERS

FAR LEFT: Five-year old Mary Elaine O'Hara dressed for a Halloween party, Sioux City, 1931. COURTESY BARBARA (BETZ) SWANSON

BELOW LEFT: Raymond Cusack and friend Jimmy Cobb pose with the "pushmobile" they built together, Sioux City, early 1930s. Raymond is the driver. COURTESY KAY AND BOB COACHER

BELOW: Emil Jahn, second from back, posing with some friends, Sioux City, late 1920s. Also identified is Frenchy Beucher (front seat), Clara Lang and Vera Peterson. COURTESY DONA AND JAHN HICKS

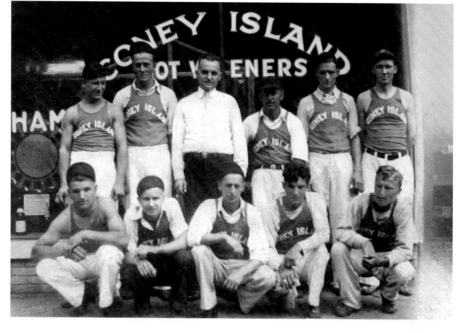

ABOVE: Wedding day photo of Dorothy Hagan, Sioux City, 1935. From left: Margaret Ryan, Maid of Honor; Mary Kelly, bridesmaid; Betty Hagan Everist, Flower Girl; and Therine Klein, bridesmaid. COURTESY ELIZABETH EVERIST

ABOVE RIGHT: State champion recreation league softball team sponsored by George Margeas and Coney Island restaurant, 510 Nebraska St., Sioux City, 1932. COURTESY STEVE MARGEAS

RIGHT: Wedding day photo of Catherine Dreves and Walter Calhoun in June 1935. The couple were married at St. Joseph's Catholic Church. COURTESY GRACE CALHOUN KAVANAUGH

FAR RIGHT: Jim Walsh and Donald Choquette, Orpheum Theatre, Sioux City, 1937. Jim did a magic trick and Donald did a Flamenco dance in an amateur talent contest at the theater. COURTESY JAMES C. WALSH

OPPOSITE: The basketball team of Tolerton and Warfield Co., Sioux City, 1930s. First three in front row are: Howard Tolles, Al Pettit and John Pettit. Bud Molden is in the back row on the far right. COURTESY LANI PETTIT

ABOVE: Riverside Park race track, between Sioux City and Riverside, about 1939. COURTESY RAYMOND LEFEBVERE

RIGHT: Morningside College String Quartet, Sioux City, about 1934. Leo Kucinski on the left. Leo is considered Sioux City's "Mr. Music" and was director of the Sioux City Symphony Orchestra, Sioux City Municipal Band and the Monahan Post band. COURTESY SIOUX CITY MUSEUM

FAR RIGHT: Harry Wallen (center), with sons Dick (left) and Raymond, pose with the horses of the White Horse Mounted Patrol, Sioux City, 1938. COURTESY BRENT WALLEN

ABOVE: Harry Wallen and his White Horse Mounted Patrol horse Silver Flash I at the stockyards, Sioux City, 1939. COURTESY BRENT WALLEN

LEFT: Ferris Wheel at Riverside Park, between Sioux City and Riverside, 1939.
COURTESY RAYMOND LEFEBVERE

Spanning 89 years...

Guarantee Roofing, Siding and Insulation Company, LLC was founded in 1926 by Ferris Skaff. During his first years the business was operated with just one truck and himself. All the work was sold by night and installed during the day.

Eventually, the business grew to the point that Mr. Skaff could hire installers to help with the jobs he sold. This was attributed to his sterling reputation and likeability.

On January 1, 1949, James (Jim) M. Yanney, Ferris Skaff's son-in-law, joined the company. At that time, the business had expanded to four company-owned trucks and cars. Jim, who previously had worked in the restaurant business, learned about roofing by working with the crews. After he became more knowledgeable, Jim began selling and building territory. He bought the company in 1970 after his father-in-law passed away. Until his death in February of 2014, Jim was active in the family business.

Guarantee, which does residential and commercial roofing, as well as windows and siding, was originally located about six blocks west of its current location at 2005 E. Fourth St., until they were forced out in dramatic fashion by a river flood in March of 1952.

In the spring of 1976, Jim and Do's daughter Charese Yanney joined the company. Pulled in by the great outdoors, the family business, and reliving sweet childhood memories of watching her father ply his craft on Sioux City's rooftops, she told her father she would be coming to work for the business started by her grandfather in 1926. Charese started in sales and learned the business by visiting job sites from beginning to completion.

Jim, Do and Charese have been active in politics and community service their entire careers. Jim and Charese are past chairs of the Chamber of Commerce and the United Way campaigns. Do, who passed away in 2008, was a co-founder of United Way's Power Lunch and Women United. Jim was a co-founder of the Better Business Bureau of Sioux City. Charese has also served with the Siouxland Initiative, Briar Cliff University, Sioux City Art Center, United Way of Siouxland, and other organizations.

Guarantee Roofing, Siding and Insulation Company, LLC is a successful business spanning 89 years and they have been involved in countless major projects including the Sioux City City Hall, Metz Baking, Port Neal Power Plant, and many schools and court houses around the area. They are proud to be part of Siouxland and will always stand as one of the area's most trusted companies for quality and workmanship.

Ferris Skaff, Founder

Palmer CANDY ®

Making Life Sweeter Since 1878

Five generations of Palmers have owned and operated the Palmer Candy Company making it the oldest family confectionary company of its size in the nation. The times have continued to change but our family's goals have stayed the same; produce quality products for our customers, provide a fulfilling work environment for our employees and affect positive change in Siouxland. We pride ourselves in being…

more than just a company, we are a family!

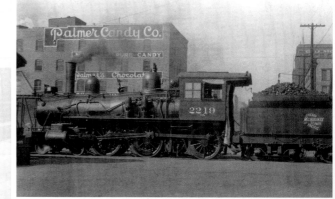

Pictured above, the Sulzbach family home
located at 621 Main St. in Sioux City.

Sulzbach family 1935 (left to right): Donald, Fred, Richard, Catherine, Robert and Rita Sulzbach.

Built on a strong foundation...

The Sulzbach Family Company is one of the few U.S. employers with four generations of one family actively involved in the business. Consisting of Sulzbach Construction Co., Sioux City Engineering Co. and Specialized Hauling, they have built a legacy in Siouxland spanning seven generations. The Sulzbach family business began with Joseph Sulzbach, who brought his family to Sioux City in 1880 and started Sulzbach Construction Co. at Sixth & Main streets. Joseph taught the brick construction trade to his son, Frederick Julius Sulzbach, who took over the family business in 1889. He expanded it into a general contracting business that covered everything from small homes to industrial plants. Frederick J. died in 1933, passing the legacy down to his son Frederick Paul Julius Sulzbach. The family business moved from Sixth & Main streets to 1500 Omaha

St. Frederick Paul's sons, Richard, Robert and Donald Sulzbach, started working in the business after World War II. They expanded into the sewer and water main construction business with Sioux City Engineering Co. and the trucking business with Specialized Hauling. Richards' two sons, Richard Jr. and James, joined the firm in 1972 and focused on trucking, concrete paving and sewer/water main construction. In 1996, after 50 years on Omaha St., the family business moved to 5000 S. Lewis Blvd. Since then, the sixth generation of Sulzbachs', Jon and Jason have taken their place in the business, with Jon's son, Christopher (the 7th generation) waiting in the wings. Over their 135-year history, the companies have grown into one of the region's largest concrete paving and sewer/water main contractors and have worked on practically every street in the Sioux City area.

Joseph Sulzbach, Founder
1829 - 1904

Fredrich Julius Sulzbach
1869 - 1933

Fredrich Paul Julius Sulzbach
1899 - 1972

Richard Paul Sulzbach
1923 -

Richard Paul Sulzbach Jr.
1948 -

Jon Paul Sulzbach
1971 -

St. Paul Lutheran Church in downtown Sioux City built by the Sulzbach Family in 1927.

Morningside Presbyterian Church on Morningside Ave. in Sioux City was built in 1924 by the Sulzbach Family.

The Fairmont Library located on Fairmont St. in Sioux City was one of the last 'prairie school style' library buildings designed by William L. Steele and built by the Sulzbach Family.

Pictured to the right in 2013, Richard Sulzbach, Richard Sulzbach Jr., Jason Sulzbach, Jon Sulzbach and Christopher Sulzbach.

FOULK BROS.
PLUMBING & HEATING

It was the turn of the 20th century when Nathaniel Cloud Foulk founded N.C. Foulk Plumbing with Lytle Construction Co. and laid the groundwork for four generations of Foulks to build on.

Born in 1876, N.C. Foulk was a lifelong resident of Sioux City. He promoted the plumbing profession as a member of the city plumbing board and worked in the business until 1951, the year he passed away. His sons, Robert L. Foulk and Billy E. Foulk, took over the company and changed the name to Foulk Bros. Plumbing & Heating, which it is still called today. During that period, the focus of the business changed toward performing more service work and working on projects for local businesses.

In 1987, they handed the reins to the third generation, William R. Foulk and Robert Foulk. Robert joined the business in the early 1960s and William R. started full time in 1970. William R.'s brother, Jon, has been an estimator in the business since the early 1980s. In 2007, Robert retired from Foulk Bros. and William R. bought out his share. William R. continues to operate Foulk Bros. Plumbing & Heating today with his son, Nathaniel J. Foulk, who joined the business full-time in 2000 and became an estimator in 2007.

In 115 years, Foulk Bros. has been in four locations: 500 block of Jackson Street, 908 Fifth St. (back and upstairs), 908 W. Seventh St., and 322 W. Seventh St., where it has been since 1972.

Over their history, Foulk Bros. Plumbing & Heating has taken pride in providing plumbing and heating services to residential and commercial customers in the Siouxland area, and working on structures, including many Sioux City landmarks that are still standing today.

Among the projects Foulk Bros. has been a part of are the Cudahy packing plant, Davidson Building, St. Thomas Episcopal Church, Cathedral of the Epiphany, Orpheum Theatre, Commerce Building, St. Vincent's Hospital, St. Luke's Regional Medical Center, many nursing homes, several area schools (public, parochial and postsecondary), including Briar Cliff University, and numerous new homes.

Foulk Bros. Plumbing & Heating has had a long and rich history in Sioux City, providing good service, doing the best job they can, and doing it with honesty. They are honored to be of service to the community - a proud tradition that was started by Nathaniel Cloud Foulk and one that the family plans to continue for generations to come.

Nathaniel Cloud Foulk,
Founder

STATEMENT
N. C. FOULK CO
— PLUMBING AND HEATING —
908 FIFTH ST.   PHONE 8-33
SIOUX CITY-1-IOWA.

$ 500
Plumbing Inspection Department
PLUMBING LICENSE
Sioux City, Iowa.   Nov 18
Received of *Robert LeRoy Foulk*
Five   Dollars
In payment of
Plumbing Inspector

State of Iowa
CITY OF SIOUX CITY
WOODBURY COUNTY

Plumber's License

To All Whom These Presents Shall Come, Greeting:

Know ye, that Mr. ROBERT LE ROY FOULK *has submitted to the examination required by the Board of Examiners, for Plumbers, as provided for in Chapter 378, 38th G. A., and having passed said examination to the satisfaction of said Board, is hereby declared to be*

Frank A. Peavy

Serving Sioux City
Since 1884

SECURITY NATIONAL BANK
SIOUX CITY • AKRON • MAPLETON • MOVILLE • LAWTON

SueBee®
America's Honey™

The year was 1921. Five beekeepers located near Sioux City, Iowa, got together and formed the Sioux Honey Association. They shared equipment, marketing and processing facilities. Sue Bee Honey was born. The rest is history.

In the early days honey was marketed under the "Sioux Bee" label, but the name was changed in 1964 to "Sue Bee" to reflect the correct pronunciation more clearly. Over time other lines of honey were added, including Clover Maid, Aunt Sue, Natural Pure and North American brands.

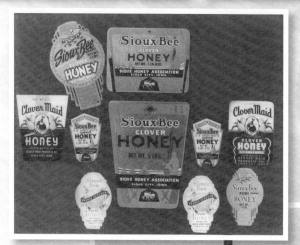

Today membership includes approximately 300 members from locations around the country. Collectively, around 40 million pounds of honey are produced each year. Sue Bee Honey is processed in plants located in Sioux City, Iowa; Anaheim, California; and Elizabethtown, North Carolina.

Today, Sue Bee Honey's global presence extends to the Middle East, Far East, Europe, and South and Central America. It continues to be a leader in the honey industry with state-of-the-art facilities and environmental awareness. Sioux Honey Association is a green company, which means our products and containers are safe for the environment and we strive to protect our ecosystem through recycling and innovative engineering.

Sue Bee Honey is proud of its long and successful history of providing one of the world's purest foods to customers around the world.

COOPERATIVE FIELD DAY • **SIOUX CITY, IOWA** • **JUNE 7, 1940**
Vocational Agriculture Instructors of Western Iowa and Northeastern Nebraska
SPONSORED BY
Producers Commission Company, Sioux City Milk Producers Cooperative Association, Progressive Farmers Cooperative Association, Farmers Union Commission Company, American Cooperative Serum Company, Sioux Honey Association, Farmers Union Cooperative Brokerage, Equity Union Creameries, and Omaha Bank for Cooperatives

The Sioux City Journal.

THERE CAN BE BUT TWO PARTIES, PATRIOTS AND TRAITORS.—Douglas.

OL. I.　　　　　　　SIOUX CITY, IOWA, SATURDAY. AUGUST 20, 1864.　　　　　　　NUMBER

Sioux City Journal	The Sioux City Journal	Poetry.
BAUGH, Publisher and Proprietor,	JOE V BAUGH. Editor	THE PRETTIEST HAND.

Mere Mention

"Madam, never mind them," said Mrs. Smith, as the woman placed her hands upon their heads. "Ed. and Kate," she continued, "go and be dressed--go this instant ot I'll whip you."

The children did not heed the mother, and the woman seemed her presence.

"Were you acquainted with Mr Robert Dupue's family? They have the same name as yourself," she eagerly inquired.

"Yes, quite well," she answered quietly.

"And is the old gentleman still living?" Mrs. Smith earnestly asked, and continued. "I have not heard fr— m in a long time."

We love women as women love all the better for their weakness.

VALUE the friendship of him who in the storm

Delivering news and information to Siouxland since 1864.

SIOUX CITY
JOURNAL
COMMUNICATIONS

INDEX